THE WORLD OF
Nature

THE WORLD OF
Nature

CLIVEDEN PRESS

Contents

Above: Freshwater insects are eaten by small fishes such as minnows. They in turn are eaten by larger fishes such as trout, as well as by birds like the kingfisher. This is a simple food chain.

The Balance of Nature

In the wild, plants and animals depend on each other for survival. Most plants make their own food with the help of energy from the sun. Animals, on the other hand, must eat plants or other animals to obtain the energy they need. The process by which energy is passed from one creature to another is called a food chain. Thus plants use the sun's energy to produce food from simple materials. Animals called herbivores eat the plants, and they themselves are eaten by carnivorous animals. If the numbers in any part of the chain rise or fall dramatically, this affects other links in the chain. Thus if a crop fails, the herbivores starve and fewer predators will survive. This is part of the process called the balance of nature.

Food chains are not always as simple as this. The carnivore may eat many types of prey and may itself be eaten by several other types of predator. When several food chains become interconnected in this way they form a food web.

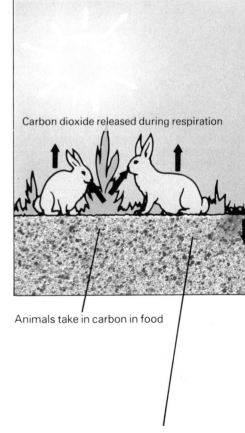

Carbon dioxide released during respiration

Animals take in carbon in food

Bacteria return carbon to soil

Below: When rabbits eat plants they take in carbon but, like all living things, they release it as carbon dioxide when they breathe out. Plants take carbon dioxide in again when they photosynthesize, and in this way the carbon is recycled.

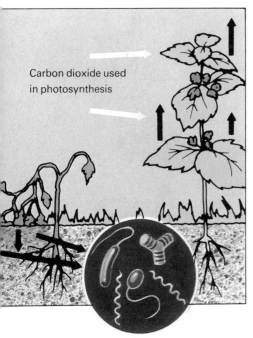

Carbon dioxide used in photosynthesis

Right: The mongoose is skilled at catching wary prey such as the black rat. It helps keep down the numbers of rats and acts as a natural 'control' agent.

Animal Populations

The numbers of animals and plants remain fairly constant from year to year. There are several factors which keep their populations in check. First the amount of food available is often limited, so the more animals there are, the less food there is to go round. If the numbers of an animal suddenly increase for some reason then the numbers of its predators soon increase as well. This gradually brings the numbers down again.

Sometimes the controls fail and numbers of a species increase unchecked. If they affect man they are called pests. In many cases man has upset the balance of nature and brought about the population explosion without realizing it.

Many insects feed on plants, but will often feed on only a few species. In the wild, the plants are generally spaced out. This spacing out helps to keep the insect population at a steady level.

But if the insect finds an area where its foodplant is abundant its numbers will soon rise. Man often grows vast areas of crops for food. As a result those insects that can eat the crop benefit and soon become pests.

Above: The Colorado beetle can become a serious pest of man's crops. It is particularly fond of potatoes and if not controlled can devastate a whole harvest.

Man often controls pests by spraying them with chemicals. But sometimes he can use natural agents as a form of biological control. Rabbits have been controlled by the introduction of a disease called myxomatosis which is transmitted by fleas. In recent years, however, many rabbits have become immune to myxomatosis.

Ichneumon wasps also make good agents of control since they lay their eggs in other insects and eventually kill them.

The Hidden Past

Fossils are evidence found in rocks of animals and plants which once lived on Earth. They range from animal footprints to animal bones, plants turned to stone and insects preserved in amber.

Why Fossils are Important

Fossils occur in rocks all over the world. Because rock layers are folded and pushed upwards, fossils of seashells are found even at the tops of mountains. The study of fossils helps geologists to date rocks. It also helps us to understand the evolution of plants and animals throughout Earth history.

The pictures above show how a fossil is formed. When an animal dies (1), it must be buried quickly in underwater sediments. The flesh soon decays, but the bones survive (2).

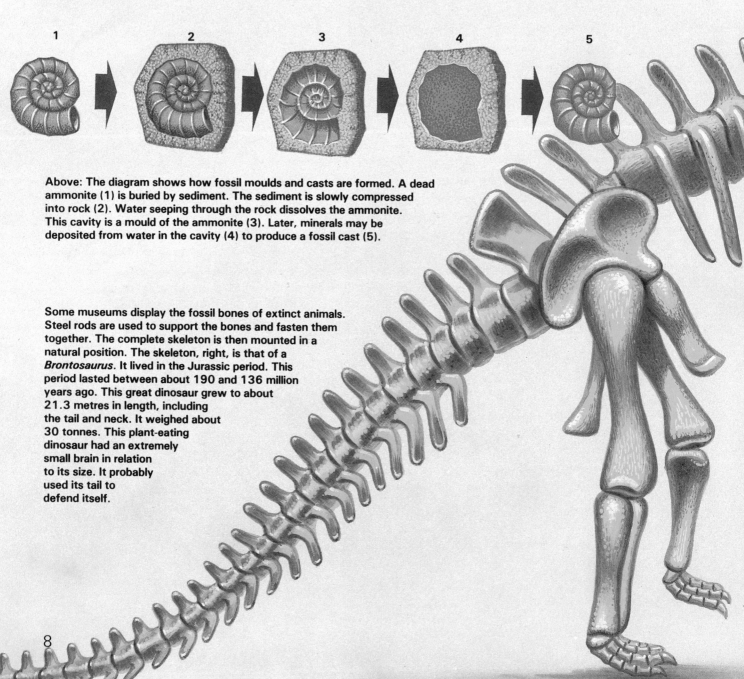

Above: The diagram shows how fossil moulds and casts are formed. A dead ammonite (1) is buried by sediment. The sediment is slowly compressed into rock (2). Water seeping through the rock dissolves the ammonite. This cavity is a mould of the ammonite (3). Later, minerals may be deposited from water in the cavity (4) to produce a fossil cast (5).

Some museums display the fossil bones of extinct animals. Steel rods are used to support the bones and fasten them together. The complete skeleton is then mounted in a natural position. The skeleton, right, is that of a *Brontosaurus*. It lived in the Jurassic period. This period lasted between about 190 and 136 million years ago. This great dinosaur grew to about 21.3 metres in length, including the tail and neck. It weighed about 30 tonnes. This plant-eating dinosaur had an extremely small brain in relation to its size. It probably used its tail to defend itself.

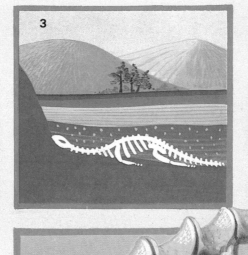

The sediments are pressed into hard rock. Minerals penetrate the buried bones, turning them into stone (3). Millions of years later, the rocks are raised up and worn down, revealing the fossil (4).

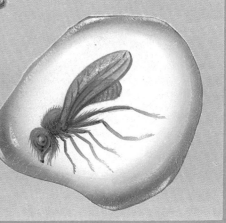

Right: Some fossils consist of the actual remains of ancient organisms. For example, insects may be trapped in sticky resin from ancient trees. The resin hardens into amber.

A person compared in size with Brontosaurus

The Formation of Fossils

For fossils to form, the remains of animals and plants must be buried quickly. Otherwise, they would rot on the surface. Burial usually takes place in the mud, silt and sand on sea, lake and river beds. After burial, the flesh of a dead animal usually decays. Hard parts, such as bones and shells, are preserved. The sediments are gradually turned into solid rock. Water seeping through the rock often deposits minerals in the pores of bones and shells, slowly turning them into stone. Sometimes, every tiny molecule of a buried log is replaced by minerals. This process forms *petrified* logs. Leaves preserved in rocks sometimes form thin films of carbon which show the shape of the leaf.

Other fossils are moulds or casts of the original hard parts (see the diagrams on the facing page). A few fossils include the actual bodies of animals, such as woolly mammoths which lived 30,000 years ago. These have been preserved in the frozen ground of Siberia. But such fossils are extremely rare.

9

Animals of Long Ago

Animals have lived on Earth for millions of years. Scientists know about them because their remains are found embedded in rocks, turned to stone. These stony remains are called *fossils*.

Nobody knows exactly when life first appeared, because there are very few fossils older than about 570 million years, the start of what is called the *Palaeozoic Era*. Palaeozoic comes from Greek words meaning 'old life'. Scientists can put approximate dates to fossils because they can work out the age of the rocks in which they are found. Fossils show how plants and animals have changed, or evolved, throughout the Earth's long history.

The Pageant of Life

The first animals were *invertebrates*, animals that have no backbones, and they lived in the sea. They were soft, primitive creatures, rather like the jellyfish and sponges of today. The first animals with backbones – *vertebrates* – appeared about 450 million years ago. They were primitive forms of fish. After a long time some fish became able to breathe air and developed lungs (there are still some lungfishes today). From them came the first animals that could live both on land and in water. These *amphibians* were the ancestors of present-day frogs. They lived about 350 million years ago.

Many kinds of life evolved on land, including insects and reptiles. By about 200 million years ago giant reptiles, the dinosaurs, ruled the Earth. They died out suddenly, about 65 million years ago. By then birds and mammals had evolved, and mammals became the dominant animals. Man is one of the most recent mammals to evolve. Our ancestors appeared about two million years ago.

Below: Some of the dinosaurs, the giant reptiles which dominated the Earth for millions of years. Alamosaurus was one of several huge beasts feeding only on plants, while Tyrannosaurus was a fierce, meat-eating predator. By contrast, Compsognathus was about the size of a turkey.

Tyrannosaurus

Compsognathus

Below: A panorama of life through prehistoric time, from the first forms of life in the sea, through the age of the dinosaurs, to the present-day age of mammals.

PALAEOZOIC ERA 570–230 million years ago

Below: The flying creature in the picture was Archaeopteryx. This strange animal may have been the world's first bird. It lived 150 million years ago in parts of Europe. Scientists now think that its primitive wings were not strong enough to lift it far off the ground, so it may have hopped and fluttered instead.

Archaeopteryx

Alamosaurus

Triceratops

Scolasaurus

MESOZOIC ERA 230–65 million years ago

CENOZOIC ERA 65 million years ago to present

Records in Nature

Californian redwood

HIGHEST MOUNTAINS (metres)

Everest, Asia, 8,863

Aconcagua, S. America, 6,960

Mt McKinley, N. America, 6,193

Kilimanjaro, Africa, 5,888

Mont Blanc, Europe, 4,810

Mt Kosciusko, Australia, 2,233

Ben Nevis, UK, 1,343

Above: During the Earth's long history, many mountain ranges have been created by movements in the rocks, and then gradually worn away by water, wind and ice. The highest peaks today are in the youngest mountain ranges – the Himalayas, Andes, Rockies and Alps. There may well have been higher mountain peaks millions of years ago.

There is a great range in the size of living things. At one end of the scale there are viruses – organisms on the very borders of life – which are too small to be seen without the aid of powerful electron microscopes. At the other extreme there is the blue whale which can weigh over 120 tonnes, and the Californian redwood tree which grows as high as a 35-storey building.

The life-span of living things also varies greatly. Small insects, such as the mayfly, have an adult life-span which can be measured in days or even hours, while the tortoise may live for 150 years or more. Some plants, especially trees, live far longer. There are giant sequoia trees in California which began life almost 4,000 years ago, and bristlecone pines which are as old as the pyramids.

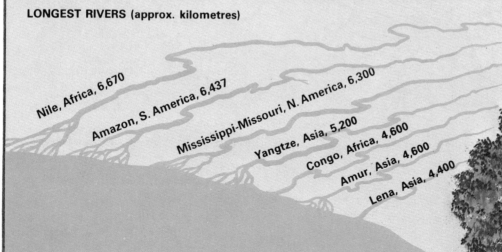

LONGEST RIVERS (approx. kilometres)

Nile, Africa, 6,670

Amazon, S. America, 6,437

Mississippi-Missouri, N. America, 6,300

Yangtze, Asia, 5,200

Congo, Africa, 4,600

Amur, Asia, 4,600

Lena, Asia, 4,400

Oak

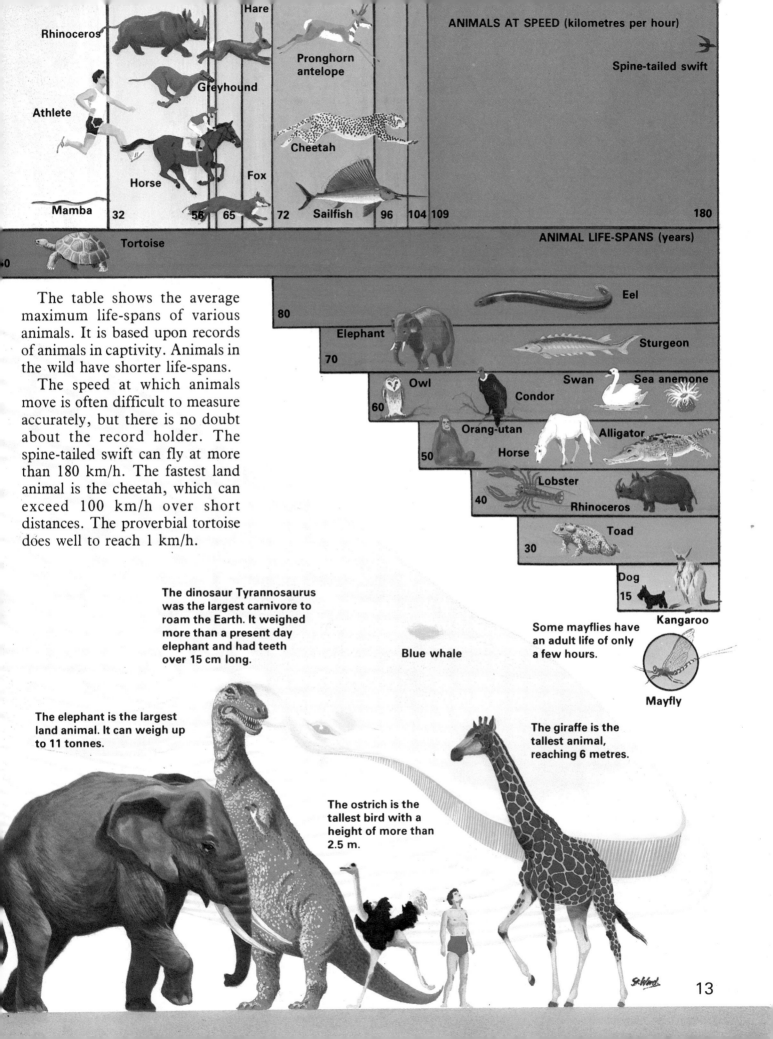

ANIMALS AT SPEED (kilometres per hour)

Spine-tailed swift

| Mamba | 32 | | 56 | 65 | 72 | Sailfish | 96 | 104 | 109 | | 180 |

Rhinoceros
Hare
Athlete
Greyhound
Pronghorn antelope
Horse
Fox
Cheetah

ANIMAL LIFE-SPANS (years)

Tortoise

The table shows the average maximum life-spans of various animals. It is based upon records of animals in captivity. Animals in the wild have shorter life-spans.

The speed at which animals move is often difficult to measure accurately, but there is no doubt about the record holder. The spine-tailed swift can fly at more than 180 km/h. The fastest land animal is the cheetah, which can exceed 100 km/h over short distances. The proverbial tortoise does well to reach 1 km/h.

Eel

80

Elephant

70

Sturgeon

Owl

60

Condor

Swan

Sea anemone

Orang-utan

50

Horse

Alligator

Lobster

40

Rhinoceros

Toad

30

Dog

15

Kangaroo

The dinosaur Tyrannosaurus was the largest carnivore to roam the Earth. It weighed more than a present day elephant and had teeth over 15 cm long.

Blue whale

Some mayflies have an adult life of only a few hours.

Mayfly

The elephant is the largest land animal. It can weigh up to 11 tonnes.

The giraffe is the tallest animal, reaching 6 metres.

The ostrich is the tallest bird with a height of more than 2.5 m.

13

The Plant Kingdom

There are nearly half a million species of plants on the earth. With the exception of some primitive types, they all need three basic ingredients to survive: air, light and water. Plants are found in almost every type of habitat, including most of the surface waters of the world's rivers, lakes and oceans. Most species live in temperate and tropical regions but plants are extremely adaptable, and have even conquered such inhospitable environments as hot mineral springs and dry deserts with little rainfall.

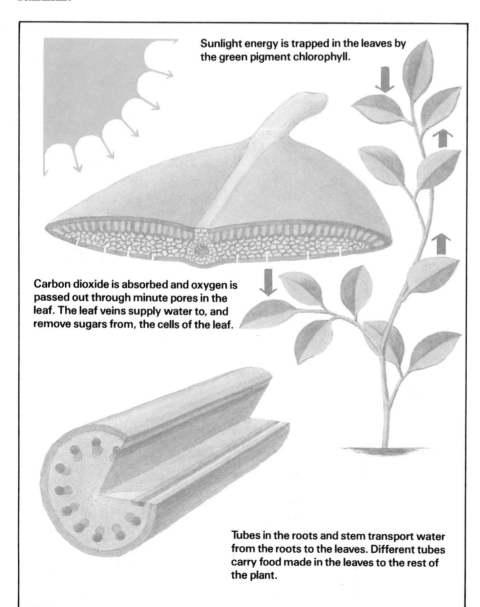

Sunlight energy is trapped in the leaves by the green pigment chlorophyll.

Carbon dioxide is absorbed and oxygen is passed out through minute pores in the leaf. The leaf veins supply water to, and remove sugars from, the cells of the leaf.

Tubes in the roots and stem transport water from the roots to the leaves. Different tubes carry food made in the leaves to the rest of the plant.

How Plants Live

Although there is a great variety in the shape, size and appearance of plants, all of them, apart from fungi and bacteria, make their own food using simple raw materials and energy from the sun. They trap the sun's rays using the green pigment chlorophyll, and combine water and carbon dioxide (a gas present in the air) to make simple sugars. They also release oxygen into the air — which all living things need for respiration. This process, known as photosynthesis, is vital to the survival of all life on earth.

Plants include some of the smallest things as well as the largest. The surface waters of ponds and lakes teem with microscopic algae, many of which exist as just a single cell. By contrast, the giant redwood trees of California may grow over 90 metres tall.

Some plants reproduce so rapidly that new individuals are produced within minutes by simple division, whereas the bristlecone pine trees live to be more than 3,500 years old. Each year they still produce a new crop of seedlings.

Almost all types of plants are eaten by one species of animal or another. Animals that eat plants are called herbivores, and they include such creatures as cows and locusts. Other animals eat only meat and these are called carnivores. However, the animals that they prey upon will have eaten plants. If it were not for plants, animal life could not exist on earth.

Right: This evolutionary 'tree' shows how the different groups of plants have evolved throughout the geological ages.

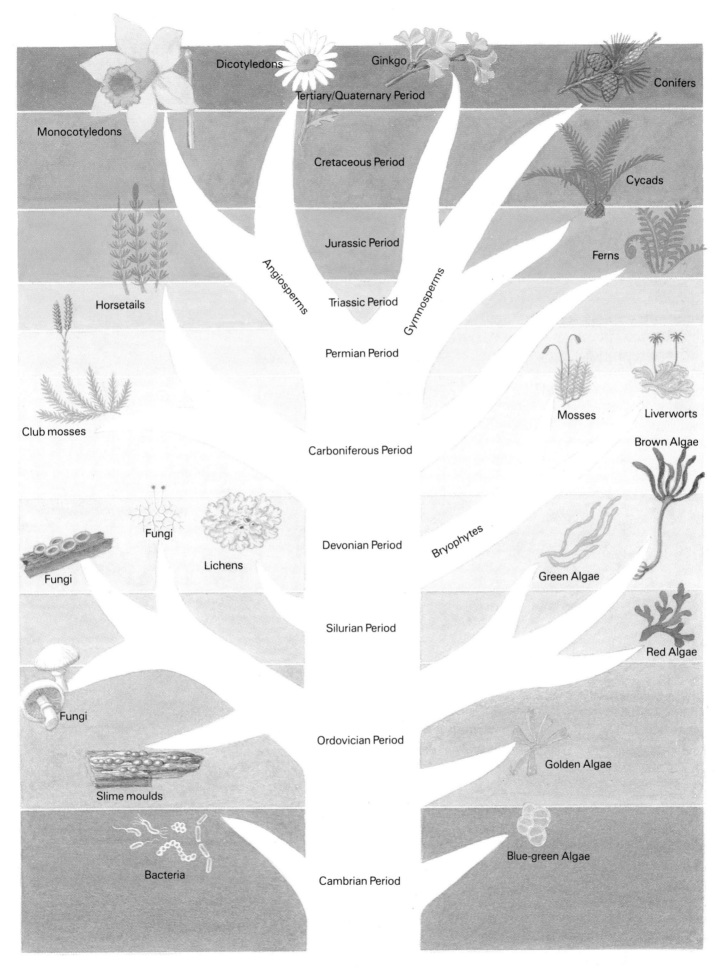

Dicotyledons

Ginkgo

Conifers

Tertiary/Quaternary Period

Monocotyledons

Cretaceous Period

Cycads

Jurassic Period

Angiosperms

Ferns

Horsetails

Triassic Period

Gymnosperms

Permian Period

Mosses

Liverworts

Club mosses

Carboniferous Period

Brown Algae

Fungi

Lichens

Devonian Period

Bryophytes

Green Algae

Fungi

Silurian Period

Red Algae

Fungi

Ordovician Period

Golden Algae

Slime moulds

Bacteria

Blue-green Algae

Cambrian Period

15

Lowly Plants

The lowly plants have existed on earth for much longer than the flowering plants we grow in our gardens. Many have remained almost unchanged for millions of years. They generally have a simple structure and, with the exception of ferns, do not have supporting fibres. This means that they cannot grow to any great size.

Most of the lowly plants contain the green pigment chlorophyll. This helps them to trap sunlight energy and make their own food. The exceptions are the bacteria and fungi which have to use other sources of food such as the dead bodies of plants or animals, and are responsible for decay.

Advanced plants mostly have flowers and produce seeds in order to reproduce. Lowly plants, however, often reproduce by means of spores. The bacteria and many of the algae reproduce by simple division, and like the rest of the lowly plants they need damp conditions.

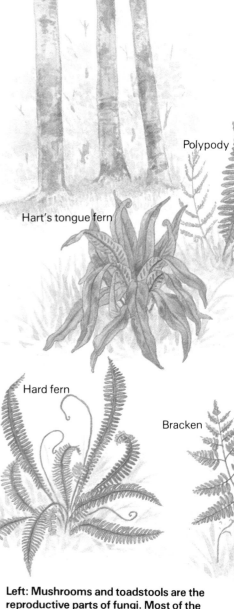

Polypody

Hart's tongue fern

Hard fern

Bracken

Dryad's saddle

Chanterelle

Horn of plenty

Fly agaric

Stinkhorn

Death cap

Puff balls

The sickener

Left: Mushrooms and toadstools are the reproductive parts of fungi. Most of the fungus lives underground forming a complex web of thread-like strands called a mycelium.

The spores of fungi are always present in the air. They grow and thrive when food, such as bread, is left in damp conditions, forming patches of mould.

Algae

Algae are the simplest forms of true plant life. They possess chlorophyll, but many contain other pigments, giving them many colours. They range from simple, single-celled plants which make ponds appear green, to immense seaweeds, several metres long.

Fungi

Unlike algae, fungi cannot make their own food and depend on a ready-made source. Many feed on dead matter and cause decay.

Lichens are strange plants which are the result of a partnership between algae and fungi. The relationship is called 'symbiotic', and both partners benefit from it. Their growth is very slow.

Mosses and Liverworts

Mosses and liverworts are simple plants which lack true roots and stems. They are restricted to damp habitats and reproduce by spores produced in capsules.

Ferns

Ferns are generally long-lived plants. They have a rootstock and a strong, supporting stem which can conduct water and dissolved food substances. This means that they can often reach a large size. They still produce spores during reproduction and depend on water for part of their life cycle.

Below: Fern spores are spread by the wind

Prothallus

Spores

New fern plant

Black spleenwort

Rustyback

Above: Ferns come in a variety of forms. Some are rooted in the soil and grow to large sizes. Others colonize walls or even grow on other plants, but all need damp conditions.

Right: Seaweeds are algae which grow on rocky shores. Mosses are common on walls and in damp places.

17

Flowers

Flowers contain the male and female cells of a plant. For successful fertilization to take place, the pollen (male cells) from one plant has to reach the ovum (female cell) of another. However, plants have one basic problem—they are rooted to the ground. To overcome this, plants have evolved all sorts of ways of transferring the pollen.

Despite their unlikely appearance, grasses are true flowering plants which produce countless thousands of minute pollen grains that are carried by the wind. Not surprisingly, most end up in the wrong place but enough reach another grass flower to ensure their survival. More typical flowers have colourful petals and often a strong smell to attract insects. In return for a meal of nectar, the insects transfer the pollen to the next flowers which they visit.

Rose

Primrose

Flower Plan

Although some species of flowers sometimes contain only the male or the female cells, most contain both but go to great lengths to prevent self-fertilization.

Despite a great variety of appearances most flowers conform to a basic plan with sepals, colourful petals, stamens which produce the male cells called pollen, and a central stigma containing the female cell or ovule.

How a plant disperses its seeds

Above: Coconut seeds float in the sea.

Above: Willowherb seeds are carried by the wind

Above: Burdock seeds have hooks which catch in the feathers and fur of animals.

Above: Poppy seeds are shaken from the pod.

The parts of a flower

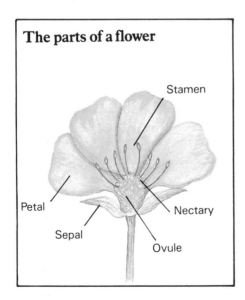

Stamen

Petal

Sepal

Nectary

Ovule

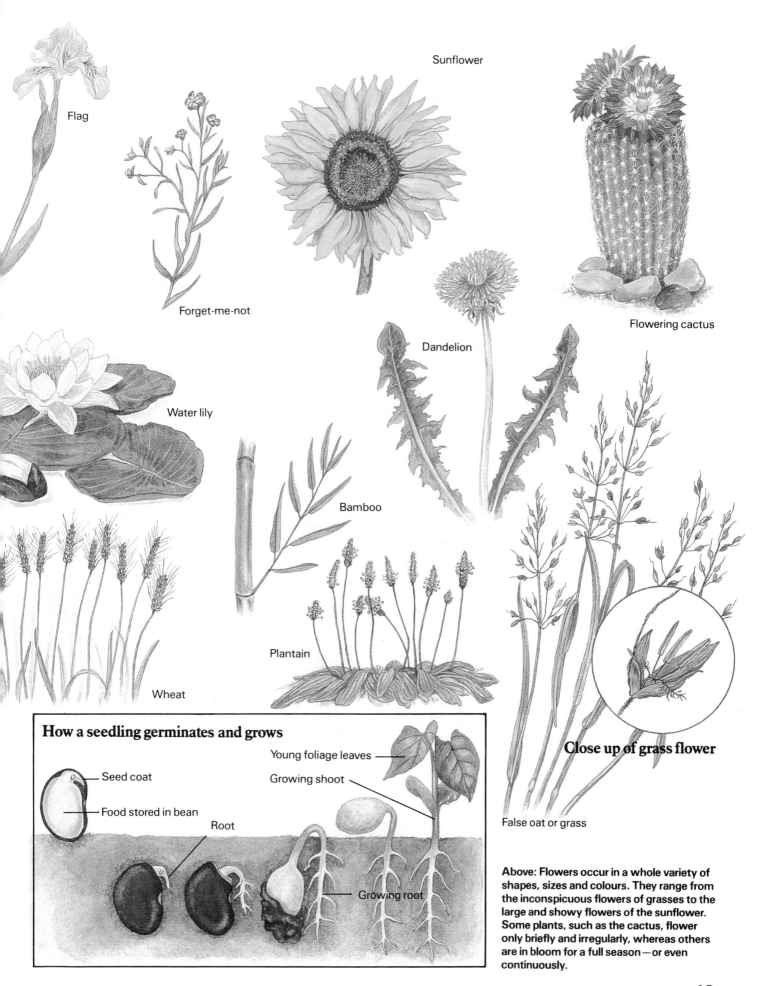

Flag

Sunflower

Forget-me-not

Flowering cactus

Water lily

Dandelion

Bamboo

Plantain

Wheat

Close up of grass flower

False oat or grass

How a seedling germinates and grows

Young foliage leaves

Growing shoot

Seed coat

Food stored in bean

Root

Growing root

Above: Flowers occur in a whole variety of shapes, sizes and colours. They range from the inconspicuous flowers of grasses to the large and showy flowers of the sunflower. Some plants, such as the cactus, flower only briefly and irregularly, whereas others are in bloom for a full season—or even continuously.

Trees

Trees, woods and forests cover nearly one quarter of the earth's surface. They are a very important part of our environment, for they provide food, homes and shelter for a great variety of other living creatures. The key feature of all trees is their central woody stem or trunk. This grows as the tree grows, and provides support and protection.

Trees can broadly be split into those which drop their leaves each year (called deciduous trees) and those which do not (called evergreens). Many evergreens bear their seeds in cones and have needle-like leaves; these trees are called conifers. There are also some broadleaved trees, such as holly, which do not shed their leaves each autumn.

Palms are a special group of trees. Although they are deciduous, they are placed in a group of plants called monocotyledons, the group which also includes the grasses.

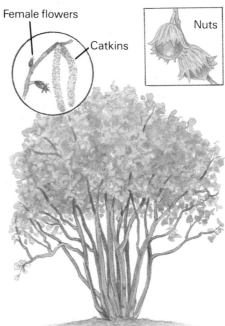

Above: The hazel is a deciduous tree. It has tiny female flowers, and male catkins which produce pollen. The seeds are encased in a tough shell, or nut.

Right: By counting the rings on a cross-section through a trunk you can estimate the age of a tree. Each ring roughly corresponds to a year's growth.

Below: There are many different types of tree throughout the world. Here are some typical species.

How Trees Grow

As well as providing support for the tree, the trunk carries the water supply for the leaves of the tree. Although the centre of the trunk is usually tough and woody, the outer tissues consist of tubes through which water is transported from the roots to the leaves. Some of this tissue also transports food from the leaves down to the roots and other parts of the tree. The trunk tissues are protected by the bark. If this is damaged, the tree may die.

Leaves are the vital life-supply for all plants. They produce food by photosynthesis, using the energy of sunlight to combine water and carbon dioxide. There are many different shapes of leaves, but all are designed to make best use of the available light.

In some parts of the world, the climate does not change during the year and the tree grows continuously. But elsewhere the climate varies, with either cold and hot seasons or dry and wet

periods. The tree grows best in favourable conditions and, as a result, we can see growth rings in the trunk, each dark ring corresponding to a year's growth. In a good year the ring is thicker than in a poor year. By counting the number of rings, the age of the tree can be worked out.

In order that trees may reproduce, the female part of the flower must first be pollinated. In some trees, male and female parts are in the same flower. In others, they are in separate flowers or, sometimes, on separate male and female trees, such as holly.

Above: The spruce is a conifer with tiny flowers. The fertilized seeds grow and ripen in cones.

Right: An oak tree supports a whole community of plants and animals. Some animals feed on its leaves or acorns while others in turn prey upon them. Many beetles and fungi feed on the decaying wood and leaves.

Cone

21

Wonders of the Plant World

In the world of nature the Plant Kingdom has many unusual and fascinating species. From plants which can only be seen with the aid of a microscope to plants taller than a house, the Plant Kingdom is full of wonders.

We only have to think of fungi, those peculiar plants which can grow without the aid of sunlight and seem to pop out of the ground overnight, to realize that some plants are very odd. However, as we shall see, there are others which can confuse scientists even more!

Diatoms

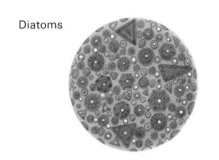

Volvox

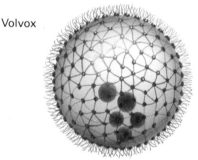

Lichen   Algae cells   Fungal hyphae

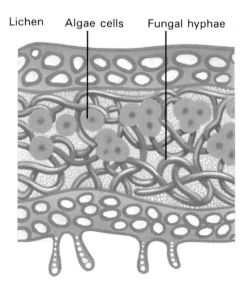

Left: Diatoms and colonies of single-celled algae like Volvox can move freely about in the water.

Right: This cross section through a plant stem shows how its water and minerals are absorbed by the suckers of mistletoe. Mistletoe grows on trees such as poplars.

Bottom left: Lichens are unusual plants made up of single-celled algae sandwiched between a fungus.

Lowly Plants

One of the ways that we normally use to tell animals from plants is by the fact that animals can move about, while plants stay fixed in one place. But among the group of primitive plants called the algae there are several species that can actually move about on their own.

Diatoms are tiny algae living within a silica shell, which can glide about in the water. Volvox is a plant which consists of a group of single-celled algae each of which has tiny hairs. By beating these Volvox can also move about in the water.

Flowering Plants

Among the flowering plants there are also many unusual species. Although most flowering plants

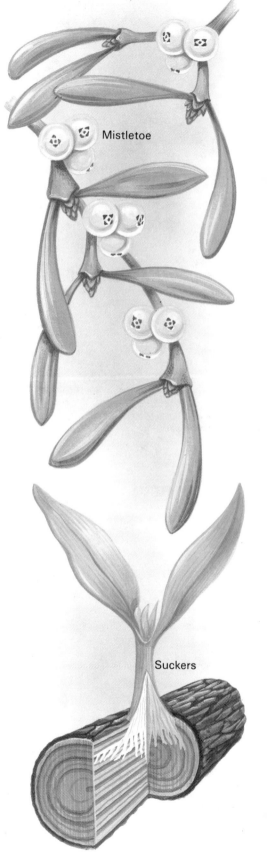

Mistletoe

Suckers

make their own food by using the energy of sunlight trapped in their leaves, there are some kinds which 'steal' the minerals and food substances from other plants.

Dodder is a twining, parasitic plant whose stem sends suckers into the host plant.

Mistletoe is known as a partial parasite. It can make its own food using sunlight, but first it must rob a host plant of some vital minerals.

The most unusual flowering plants are the carnivorous species.

They live in places, such as bogs, which lack the nitrogen they need for healthy growth. Therefore they catch insects and other small creatures in special traps (which are really special leaves) and absorb the nitrogen from their bodies.

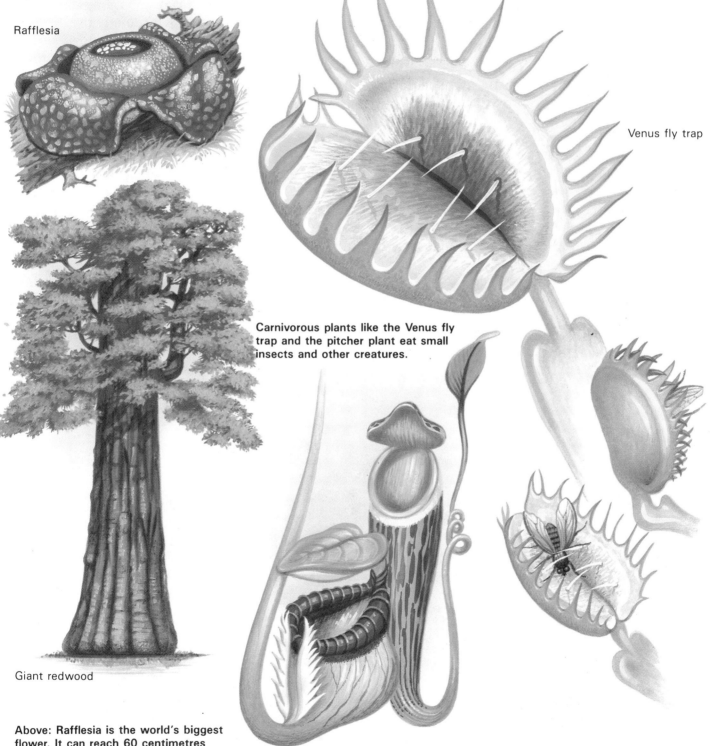

Rafflesia

Venus fly trap

Giant redwood

Carnivorous plants like the Venus fly trap and the pitcher plant eat small insects and other creatures.

Above: Rafflesia is the world's biggest flower. It can reach 60 centimetres across. Giant redwood trees can reach heights of 110 metres.

Pitcher plant

23

The Animal Kingdom

The Animal Kingdom can be divided simply into two large groups: animals without backbones (also known as invertebrates) and animals with backbones (also known as vertebrates).

Some of the more familiar invertebrate animals we see around us include insects, crabs, worms and spiders. Animals like cats and dogs, snakes, frogs, birds and fishes belong to the other group, the vertebrates.

Vertebrate animals are generally much bigger than invertebrate animals. They also *seem* to be more common. However, there are many more invertebrate animals in the world than there are vertebrate animals. About 95 per cent of the whole Animal Kingdom is composed of invertebrate animals. Many of them spend much of their lives hidden from view, however — in the soil, in the sea or concealed among the bark of trees.

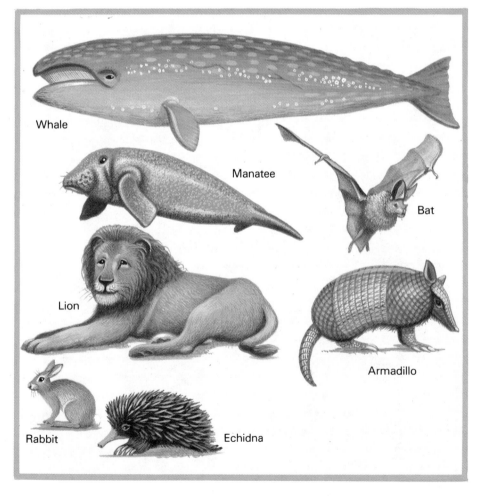

Whale

Manatee

Bat

Lion

Armadillo

Rabbit

Echidna

Animal Classification

Animals (and plants) are grouped together according to particular features that they have in common. We have already seen how animals can be grouped into vertebrates and invertebrates. The next major division within the Animal Kingdom is the phylum. Animals within a phylum also share many features in common. For instance, the animals grouped together in the Phylum Arthropoda all have a tough, external skeleton called an exoskeleton, and jointed legs.

Within each phylum the animals are arranged in separate classes. Animals within each class share many common features of body structure. Thus, within the Phylum Arthropoda, the Class Insecta includes all those animals whose bodies are divided into three parts and bear three pairs of legs — in other words, the insects.

The next division, within the classes, is the order. Within each order are usually a number of families. Families contain animals which are similar in many ways. In the world of birds, all the tits (blue tit, coal tit and so on) are grouped together in the same family.

The next division is the genus. The final division is the species. All the species within a particular genus are basically alike. It is only animals of the same species breeding together which can produce young animals capable of themselves breeding.

Right: This family tree of the Animal Kingdom shows the main groups of animals which have appeared on earth.

Left: Although they all look quite different, all these animals are mammals. Their bodies bear fur and they suckle their young.

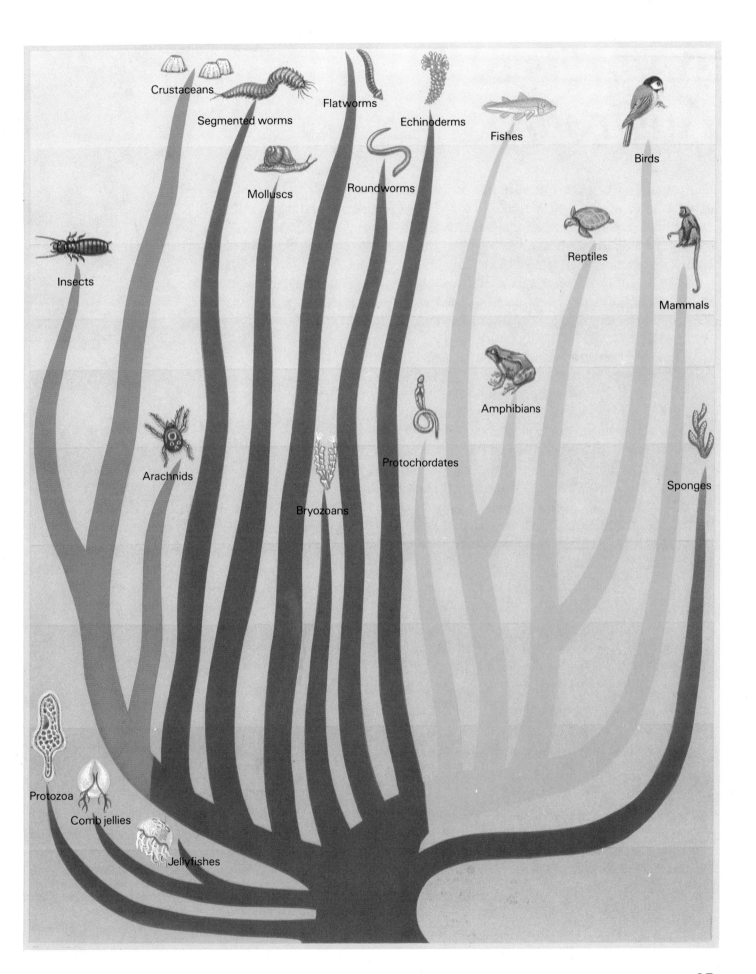

Crustaceans

Segmented worms

Flatworms

Echinoderms

Fishes

Birds

Molluscs

Roundworms

Insects

Reptiles

Mammals

Arachnids

Amphibians

Protochordates

Bryozoans

Sponges

Protozoa

Comb jellies

Jellyfishes

Animals of Australia

Australia is a huge continent in the South Pacific. Together with other islands such as New Zealand and New Guinea, it forms an area called Australasia. Naturalists have always been fascinated by the wildlife of Australia, for many of the animals there are found nowhere else in the world today.

Many millions of years ago the land masses of the Australasian region were connected to the rest of the world. All the animals roamed freely across the continents because at that time they were not separated by great oceans.

Then, the continents began to drift apart. Australia and the other countries of Australasia slowly moved towards the South Pole. Now, all the kinds of animals which were living there became separated, or isolated, from all the other countries of the world by thousands of kilometres of ocean.

Before the drift began most of the mammals were of the kind called marsupials. They had pouches in which the young developed. There were also some other, even stranger, mammals called monotremes. They laid eggs. Cut off from the rest of the world, Australia's mammals developed into many species quite different from the mammals which later arose in other parts of the world.

Cockatoo

Bird of Paradise

Bee-eater

Above: Some of Australia's birdlife is also very unusual. The kookaburra is related to the kingfishers. It has a very distinctive call and because of this is also known as the 'laughing jackass'. Some Australian birds, such as the bee-eater, birds of Paradise, parrots and cockatoos, are beautiful birds with extremely colourful plumage. Birds of Paradise and parrots live in dense forests, but bee-eaters prefer sandy banks and kookaburras live near water.

INTRODUCED MAMMALS

The arrival of the first men in Australia several thousand years ago caused some important changes. The earliest men brought with them domestic dogs. Some of these returned to the wild and began to prey on the marsupial mammals, which were unable to defend themselves. The later settlers brought sheep and cattle. The farmers who tended these animals drove many of the native animals off their grazing land. Other introduced mammals such as rats and rabbits also competed with the marsupials for food and territory. Today, many marsupials are in danger of extinction, and special measures have been taken to protect them.

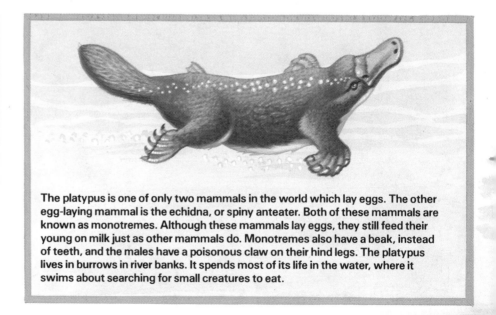

The platypus is one of only two mammals in the world which lay eggs. The other egg-laying mammal is the echidna, or spiny anteater. Both of these mammals are known as monotremes. Although these mammals lay eggs, they still feed their young on milk just as other mammals do. Monotremes also have a beak, instead of teeth, and the males have a poisonous claw on their hind legs. The platypus lives in burrows in river banks. It spends most of its life in the water, where it swims about searching for small creatures to eat.

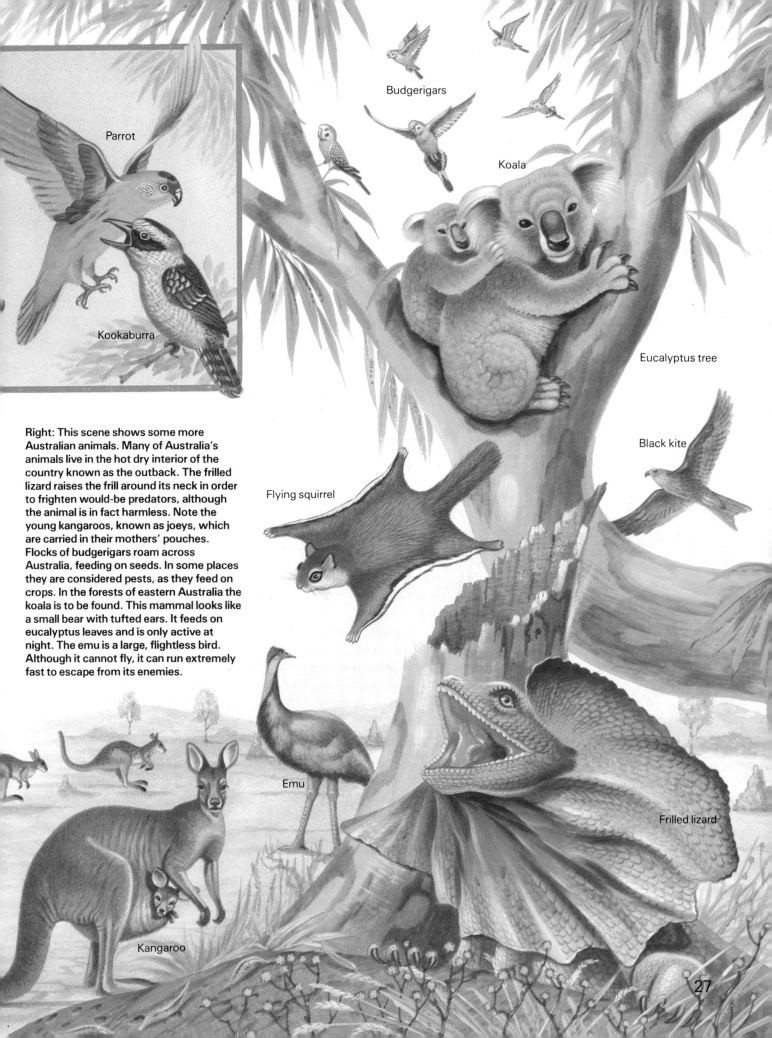

Parrot

Budgerigars

Koala

Kookaburra

Eucalyptus tree

Black kite

Flying squirrel

Right: This scene shows some more
Australian animals. Many of Australia's
animals live in the hot dry interior of the
country known as the outback. The frilled
lizard raises the frill around its neck in order
to frighten would-be predators, although
the animal is in fact harmless. Note the
young kangaroos, known as joeys, which
are carried in their mothers' pouches.
Flocks of budgerigars roam across
Australia, feeding on seeds. In some places
they are considered pests, as they feed on
crops. In the forests of eastern Australia the
koala is to be found. This mammal looks like
a small bear with tufted ears. It feeds on
eucalyptus leaves and is only active at
night. The emu is a large, flightless bird.
Although it cannot fly, it can run extremely
fast to escape from its enemies.

Emu

Frilled lizard

Kangaroo

27

Life on the African Plains

The African Plains are vast belts of grassland stretching across the continent. Some of the African Plains occur in the temperate regions of southern Africa, but most are found in the tropics. Rainfall occurs for only a short period in tropical grasslands. When it rains the grass grows high and lush. Between the rains the land looks rather barren, with few trees.

The grasses provide food for a variety of large animals such as elephants, giraffes, deer and zebra. Smaller animals like insects and snakes find shelter and food among the grasses, too.

Life on the African Plains can be harsh. The grazing animals must constantly be on the lookout for predators, and they may struggle to survive in years when droughts occur. During droughts, the grasses shrivel and die, fires are common, and even waterholes may dry up. Then, the great herds of grazing animals must often roam far in search of water and food.

Animals of the African Plains

One of the most astonishing sights in nature is to see the huge herds of animals such as wildebeest, many thousands of individuals strong, as they move slowly across the plains. Sometimes herds of different animals such as zebras and antelopes will join together for mutual protection, the whole herd alert to danger.

Few of the grazing animals compete with each other for food, for each type specializes in eating different vegetation. The tall acacia trees can only be reached by giraffes, smaller bushes are eaten by other grazers like eland, and the grasses are eaten by rhinoceroses, zebras and gazelles.

The birdlife of the African Plains includes the huge, flightless ostrich as well as birds of prey like the secretary bird, which attacks and eats snakes. Hidden among the vegetation are hordes of insects, spiders and other small creatures. These provide food for small rodents and reptiles, which themselves may fall prey to other predators.

Predators

The many herds of grazing animals provide food for the carnivorous animals of the African

Plains. The best known of these are the cats—the lions, cheetahs and leopards. Antelopes and zebras form the main food for the cats. Each of the cats has its own special way of catching food. Lions normally hunt in groups. They may lie in wait at a waterhole or surprise a herd on the open plain. Often some of the lions in the group will chase prey to where other lions are waiting.

Cheetahs rely on their great speed to catch prey. They will wait silently, crouched among the grass, until they single out a victim from the herd. Then they bound after their prey at great speed. Cheetahs can run at over 100 kilometres per hour for short distances, but they soon become exhausted and give up the chase if they have not caught their prey within about 40 metres. Leopards eat small antelopes and birds.

Once the prey is brought down and killed with a bite to the neck, it is dragged to safety and eaten. Members of a pride of lions will often feed on the prey together, the strongest individuals taking the best pieces. When the cats have had their fill, it is time for other creatures of the plains to join the feast. First to arrive will often be the hyaenas, which scrap noisily between each other over the leftovers. Then come the vultures, and finally the scavenging insects.

In the Amazon Jungle

The Amazon Jungle is part of a huge rain forest covering much of tropical South America. Rain forests are special kinds of forest. Here, the temperature is high all year round and heavy rainfall occurs frequently. These conditions are just right for rich plant growth, and within rain forests we find many kinds of luxuriant trees and other plants such as orchids, ferns and bromeliads.

LIFE IN THE JUNGLE CANOPY
Although some animals are to be found living on the floor of the rain forest, many more creatures live among the canopy. Brightly coloured birds like toucans and parrots fly among the treetops, and groups of monkeys live in noisy family groups. Here we also find the predatory animals such as snakes, and harpy eagles which swoop down to snatch birds and small monkeys in their sharp talons. Sometimes predatory cats such as jaguars also climb the trees in search of prey.

Right: The world's tropical rain forests are found in equatorial regions where the temperature is always above 18°C (65°F) and where at least 200 centimetres of rain falls each year. The world's rain forests are being destroyed as man clears them to make way for land to farm. Since 1945 over half of all the world's rain forests have been cut down.

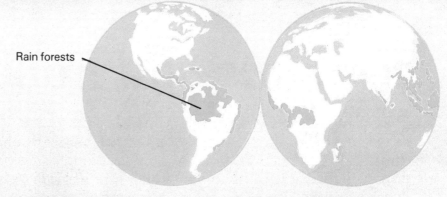

Rain forests

The trees in rain forests consist of species like ebony, teak and mahogany. They grow close together, with their upper branches thrusting towards the sky. The top-most parts of the trees form a layer known as the canopy. The leaves of the canopy layer shade most of the sunlight due to their density, and so the forest floor is gloomy, with little plant growth. Most of the other plants of the rain forest grow on the trunks and stems of the trees, about 15 metres off the ground where some sunlight still penetrates. Plants which grow on other plants are called epiphytes.

Below: Seen from the air, the Amazon rain forest appears as a dense canopy of leaves. These upper branches are the home of many animals, such as monkeys, birds and snakes. On the floor, where little light penetrates, live creatures such as huge beetles and centipedes, as well as deer and the pig-like tapir. Jaguars move stealthily among the tree roots, waiting to pounce on their prey.

Streams and Ponds

Plants and animals in streams and ponds have a very different kind of life from those on the seashore. For one thing the water is fresh. For another, the water level, though it may change according to how much rain has fallen, is much more constant than on the seashore. The plants and animals are also much more closely linked to the land around them.

Some ponds are small and shallow, and their waters are more or less stagnant. Others are deep lakes. Some are constantly enriched by material that is washed into them from streams. Plants grow in shallow mud, especially around the edges of ponds. These water weeds provide shelter for such creatures as water snails, worms, freshwater shrimps and leeches. There are also many larvae of insects such as stoneflies, mayflies and caddis flies. In deeper water there are such creatures as water-fleas (daphnia) and the fishes that feed on them.

RIVER REACHES

Rivers can be classified according to how fast the water flows through them. The water is faster and more *turbulent* (churned up) in mountainous regions, and slower and more gentle in the flat plains. The speed of the water, plus its depth and temperature, affect the type of fish found in a particular reach. For example, trout like fast, cold mountain streams, whereas bream prefer deeper and warmer slow-running rivers.

From its source to its mouth, a river can be divided into four zones, each one named after the fish most commonly found there. They are the trout, minnow, chub and bream regions.

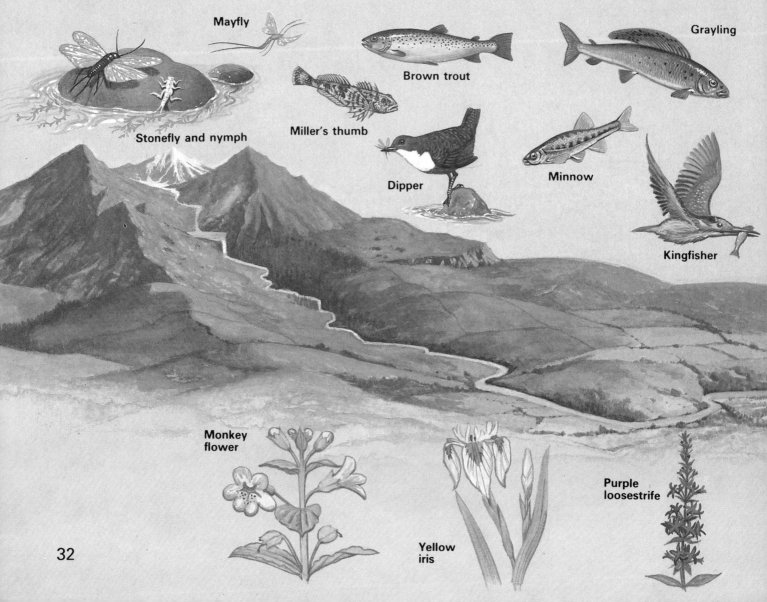

Mayfly

Stonefly and nymph

Miller's thumb

Brown trout

Dipper

Minnow

Grayling

Kingfisher

Monkey flower

Yellow iris

Purple loosestrife

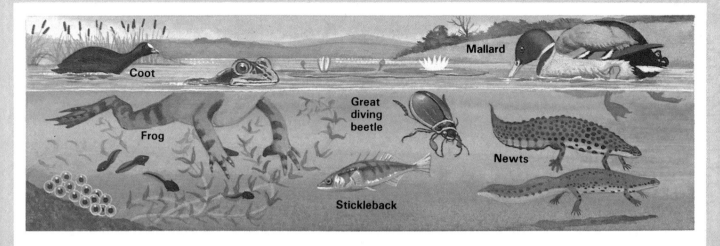

POND LIFE

However quiet a pond may look on the surface, it is a busy place under water. Frogs lay their eggs there, and the eggs hatch into wriggling, active tadpoles. The frogs' relatives, the newts, also lay their eggs in water, and the warty newts tend to stay there all the time.

The many fishes include sticklebacks. At breeding time the male stickleback builds a nest of bits of plant, in which the female lays her eggs.

Many nymphs, the young of certain insects, live in water, and so do some adults, though they have to come to the surface to breathe.

The great diving beetle, up to 40 mm long, attacks almost any living thing in the pond, including small fishes.

Water birds include ducks, swans and coots, which feed on fish and insects. The commonest duck is the mallard, which nests on shore.

Below: A panorama of the rich and varied life to be found in and close to a river, from its source in the mountains to the time it flows into the sea. The stonefly and the mayfly are two insects well known to fishermen, because they are popular food for the brown trout, which gives its name to this stretch of the river. The insects' larvae are eaten by such fish as the miller's thumb, also called the bullhead. In the same region is the dipper, a bird that stands on the stream bed watching for food, mostly insects.

In the next stretch the minnow and grayling are common fishes. The minnow is a popular food for the brightly-coloured kingfisher.

Roach are found when the stream is flowing at a moderate pace. They also feed on insect larvae, such as the young of dragonflies, and on various plants. Moorhens nest on the banks. Nearer the sea, perch are abundant, and in the river mouth such sea fishes as flounder and mullet live. Herons fish in the shallows.

Some of the wild flowers to be found in or near streams are shown along the bottom of the picture. The sea aster is a coastal plant.

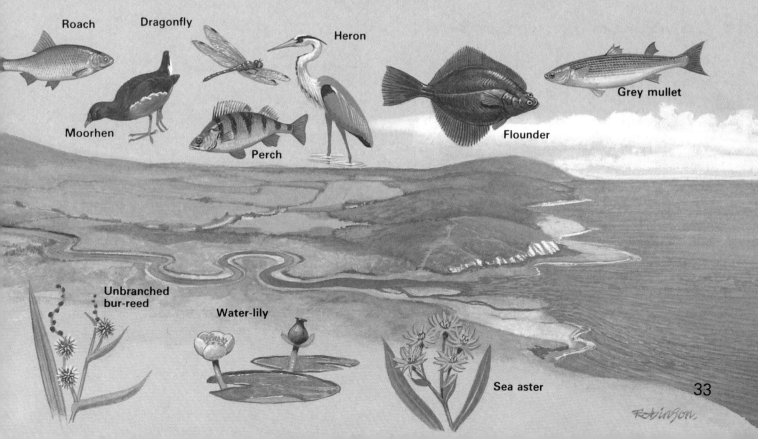

Life in the Mojave Desert

Deserts are found in parts of the world where there is very little rainfall. Most deserts are hot, dry places but some are very cold. On average, less than 25 centimetres of rain falls each year in deserts. Sometimes it may not rain in the desert at all for several years. Then torrential rain will fall, bringing floods which sweep through the desert.

Deserts are usually rocky or sandy, with little vegetation. The plants and animals which live in deserts have to find special ways of living in the harsh, dry conditions.

The Mojave Desert is in southern California, in the U.S.A. It covers an area of about 38,850 square kilometres.

Cactus

Coral snake

Animals of the Mojave Desert

As in other hot deserts, animals of the Mojave Desert have developed special methods to help them keep cool and conserve water. Many animals burrow underground by day. In the Mojave Desert the temperature may be 35°C lower underground than on the surface by day. At night, when the temperature has dropped, the animals leave their burrows to hunt for food.

Animals such as desert rats have large eyes which help them to see at night. Hunters such as snakes rely on sensing the warm bodies of their prey in order to track them down.

When desert animals must travel about during the daytime, they move very fast so that they do not remain too long in contact with the hot ground. The roadrunner uses its great speed to catch lizards and small snakes.

Plants of the Mojave Desert

The largest and most spectacular plants of the Mojave Desert are the cacti. Saguaro cacti can grow to over 16 metres in height. Cacti absorb water very quickly when it rains and then store it in their thick leaves and stems. Plants which can do this are called succulents. The creosote bush is another strange desert plant which can actually survive being dried up by the sun's rays.

When the rains come, all the desert plants quickly bloom, and seeds which had lain dormant in the ground suddenly germinate. For a short while the barren desert becomes a flower-filled landscape.

Tarantula

Animals such as the scorpion and the kangaroo rat build underground burrows.

Scorpion

Gila monster

Lanner falcon

Deserts

Rattlesnake

Horned lizard

Shovel-nose snake

Roadrunner

Jerboa

Ground squirrel

Kangaroo rat

Above: The desert is full of animal life, although most species spend the day hiding away in the shade. The map at the top shows the main deserts of the world.

Beetle

35

Ends of the Earth

The polar regions cover the most northern and most southern areas of the globe. In the northern hemisphere the polar region is called the arctic, and in the southern hemisphere it is called the antarctic. Animals that live in the polar regions have to endure some of the harshest conditions on earth. There are permanent snow and ice fields over much of the areas, and there is always the chance of a sudden icy blizzard, even in summer.

Rich Life in the Seas

Most of the land in the polar regions is either covered with snow, or is frozen just below the surface. As a result, few animals can find food here.

However, the polar seas are extremely rich in food, and provide food for birds such as penguins, and mammals such as bears, whales and seals.

Long Days and Nights

In the polar regions, the sun never climbs very high in the sky, even at the height of summer. As a result, its warming effect is never properly felt. However, throughout the summer it never sets, giving the polar inhabitants perpetual daylight.

In the winter, however, the sun only rises above the horizon each day for a few hours at most. At the poles themselves it does not rise at all for several weeks. Many of the animals move away from the poles in winter to find milder climates and more daylight.

Top left: Some animals stay and endure the arctic winter. A few, like the ptarmigan, turn white to camouflage them against the snow.

Left: In the summer, the arctic tundra is visited by many migrant birds such as waders and geese. The ptarmigan and arctic fox lose their white coloration.

Below: The dramatic antarctic is home to millions of penguins.

Birds Around the World

Birds are found all around the world, from the hottest deserts to the icy polar caps. Some are specialized and have restricted distributions. Thus, secretary birds are found only on the African Plains, and hummingbirds are found only in the Americas. Other species have wider distributions. The golden eagle, for instance, is found all over the northern hemisphere.

Birds are grouped into families which share recognizable features. Some families have representatives in all parts of the world. For example, ducks, geese and swans can be found in almost every habitat, and all share a similar appearance with webbed feet and a flattened bill. Puffins, and their relatives the auks, on the other hand, are only found in the northern hemisphere.

Nectar Eaters

Hummingbirds are a very specialized group of birds which can hover while collecting nectar from flowers. They are usually very colourful birds with iridescent plumage. Hummingbirds are only found in the Americas, with most species occurring in Central and South America.

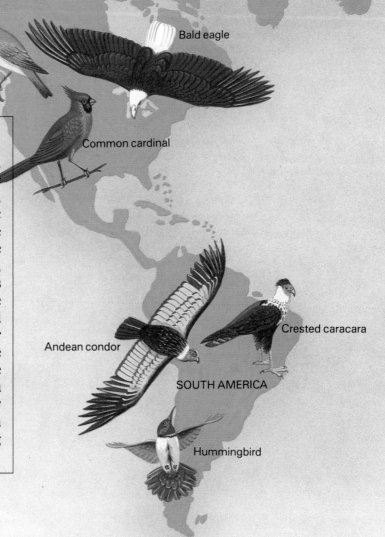

Skua

ARCTIC

Tern

Osprey

NORTH AMERICA

Red-eyed vireo

Bald eagle

Common cardinal

Andean condor

Crested caracara

SOUTH AMERICA

Hummingbird

Skua

Bird Movements

Despite their powers of flight, some birds move very little during their lives. Ptarmigan, for example, are arctic gamebirds which remain in the same habitat even under the harshest of winter conditions, and seldom fly unless disturbed. In complete contrast, albatrosses and shearwaters spend the major part of their lives at sea on the wing, ranging across the oceans of the southern hemisphere. They spend only a few short weeks ashore each year during the breeding season.

In Africa, the sunbirds have also evolved to collect nectar. They cannot hover and are not related to hummingbirds, but look remarkably similar at first glance.

Birds of Prey

Birds of prey are found all over the world. They have sharp talons which they use to grip their prey, and a hooked beak to tear the flesh. They range in size from the tiny pygmy falcon, no bigger than a sparrow, to immense eagles which can soar effortlessly for hours on end.

Some birds of prey are specialized to feed on carrion. These are the vultures and the condors. They are not very closely related, although they look similar. Condors are found only in the Americas whereas vultures only occur in Europe, Africa and Asia.

Birds of the Antarctic

The most characteristic birds of the antarctic are the penguins. These rather comical birds feed on the abundant marine life in the polar seas.

There are many different species but they all share the same characteristics. They have lost the ability to fly. Instead, they use their wings as flippers to swim, almost like flying, under water. Their feathers form a dense, insulating layer against the freezing waters and biting wind. They are an extremely successful family, and colonies often number over a million birds.

Below: Birds are found on all continents of the world.

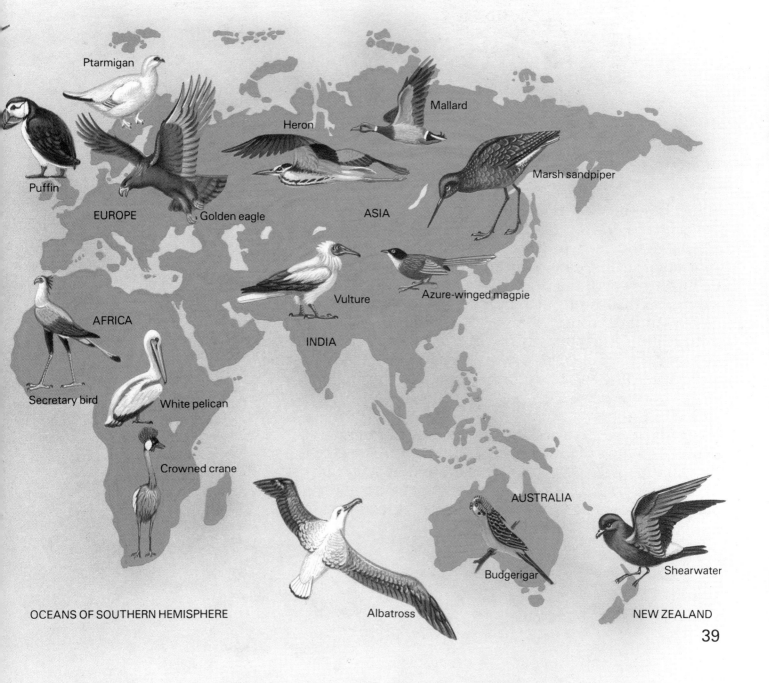

Ptarmigan

Mallard

Heron

Puffin

EUROPE

Golden eagle

ASIA

Marsh sandpiper

Vulture

Azure-winged magpie

AFRICA

INDIA

Secretary bird

White pelican

Crowned crane

AUSTRALIA

Budgerigar

Shearwater

OCEANS OF SOUTHERN HEMISPHERE

Albatross

NEW ZEALAND

Friends and Foes

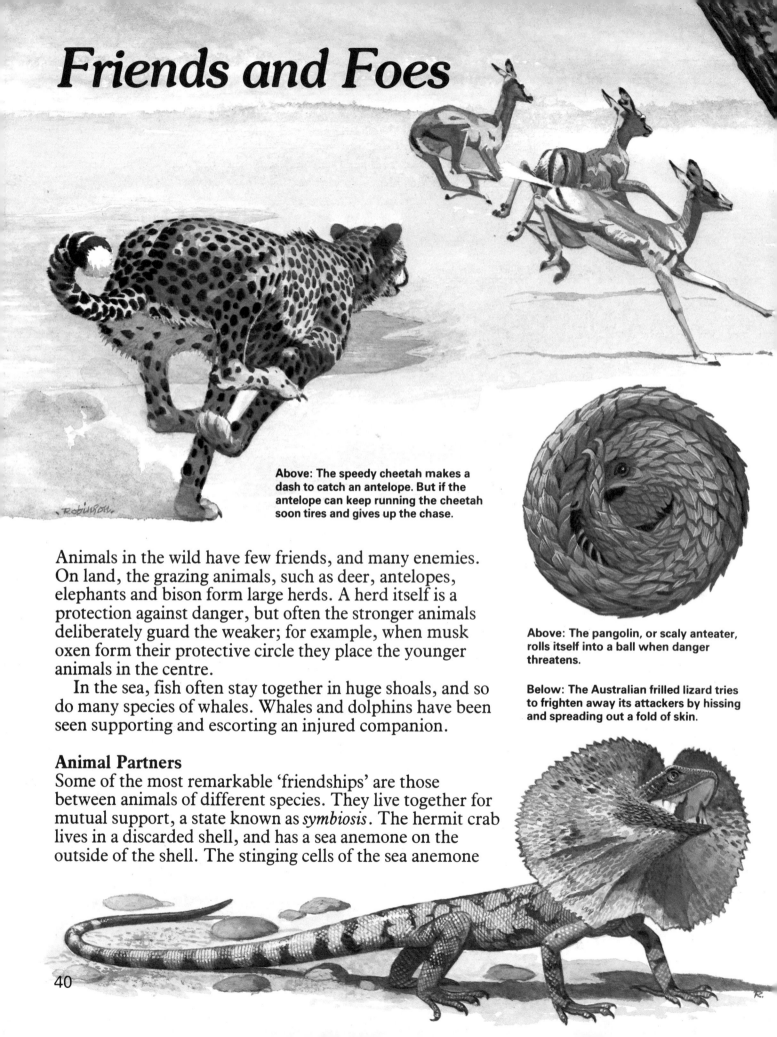

Above: The speedy cheetah makes a dash to catch an antelope. But if the antelope can keep running the cheetah soon tires and gives up the chase.

Above: The pangolin, or scaly anteater, rolls itself into a ball when danger threatens.

Below: The Australian frilled lizard tries to frighten away its attackers by hissing and spreading out a fold of skin.

Animals in the wild have few friends, and many enemies. On land, the grazing animals, such as deer, antelopes, elephants and bison form large herds. A herd itself is a protection against danger, but often the stronger animals deliberately guard the weaker; for example, when musk oxen form their protective circle they place the younger animals in the centre.

In the sea, fish often stay together in huge shoals, and so do many species of whales. Whales and dolphins have been seen supporting and escorting an injured companion.

Animal Partners

Some of the most remarkable 'friendships' are those between animals of different species. They live together for mutual support, a state known as *symbiosis*. The hermit crab lives in a discarded shell, and has a sea anemone on the outside of the shell. The stinging cells of the sea anemone

40

protect the crab, and the anemone benefits from food particles discarded by the crab. When the crab grows and moves to a bigger shell, it takes its sea anemone with it.

Little fishes known as wrasses living in the Indian and Pacific oceans act as cleaners for bigger fish. They eat parasites, such as fish-lice, on the bodies of the larger fish, which queue up to be cleaned.

When Danger Threatens

Danger in the wild comes from the *carnivores*, the flesh-eaters, who prey on the *herbivores*, the plant-eaters. The term 'carnivore' includes not only such large animals as tigers and hyenas, but also many birds which prey on small creatures such as insects.

Some animals, such as the springbok, rely on their speed to escape from danger. The hedgehog curls up, presenting a predator with an unappetising ball of prickles. Many animals have *protective coloration*: their colouring matches that of their background. For example, a white Arctic hare is hard to see against snow. Small creatures often look like something else: there are moths which resemble bird droppings, insects which look like leaves or twigs, and plaice which match the sea bed on which they lie. Many creatures, such as wasps, are harmful to eat, and have *warning coloration*, generally red or yellow and black. Other animals mimic this coloration, even though they are not unpleasant to eat; for example, hoverflies look very like wasps.

Above: Some examples of insect camouflage on a tree trunk. At the top a katydid nestles among leaves of a similar colour. The stick insect poses to look just like a twig on the side of the tree, while the treble bar moth has colouring like the trunk itself. The leaf-insect 'hides' by sitting openly on a leaf. Even bright colours can be a camouflage, as can be seen in the yellow crab spider crouched on a buttercup awaiting its prey.

Right: Oxpeckers are African starlings which spend their lives living on large animals, such as the Cape buffalo shown here. They feed on ticks and other parasites which they pull out of the animals' skin. They warn their hosts when danger is about by uttering loud cries and flying about in the air. The large animals take no notice of their companions except when they give the alarm. The birds make their nests in holes in trees, or in rocks.

Nature Trails

The best way to find out about animals and plants is to take a walk in the country, or even take a look in a town garden.

Many national parks and country parks have nature trails marked out to lead naturalists to the places where they can see the most interesting plants and animals. They often provide identification plates similar to those opposite, to help people to put a name to what they see.

Most naturalists following nature trails find that it is a good plan to take a notebook and pencil, to make a record of anything they see, and even a sketch to help identification later. Binoculars are a great help for studying birds, and a pocket magnifying glass is essential to find out the details of plants which may look alike to the casual eye.

There is another form of nature trail, too – that left by the feet of animals as they go about their daily lives. Such footprints show up best in snow, but they can also be detected in soft ground, and even in dewy grass. There are other marks, too, that betray the presence of animals, such as the claw marks which badgers leave on the trees and logs they use as scratching posts, or holes in a bank which are home to some small creatures.

The best time to see and identify tracks left by animals is when snow is on the ground. Remember animals leave slightly different marks according to the way they are moving, and this shows up clearly in snow.

Fox, trotting

Badger, bounding

Roe deer

Rabbit

Shrew

42

Oak

Birch

Lombardy
poplar

Scots pine

Larch

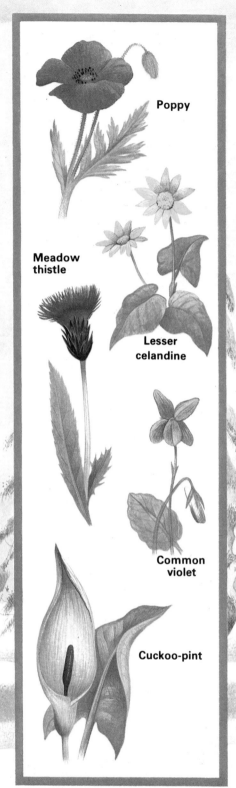

Poppy

Meadow
thistle

Lesser
celandine

Common
violet

Cuckoo-pint

Tawny
owl

Swallow

Redstart

Lapwing

Pochard

Mouse,
bounding

Rabbit,
hopping slowly

Squirrel, jumping

Stoat, bounding

Nature in the Garden

It is not always necessary to go on a nature trip to the countryside, or to the seashore, in order to find plenty of wildlife. For many of our own back gardens provide a wonderful haven for plants and animals.

Some gardens are better than others for attracting wildlife. The best ones are those with plenty of trees growing in them, and where a part of the garden is allowed to grow 'wild'. This can easily be done by sowing some wild flower seeds in a small corner, or allowing a little of the lawn to grow longer than usual.

A pond will also prove to be a welcome feature for wild animals, many of which will come to drink, feed or lay their eggs. A small pile of rocks of even just a few bricks will make a home for spiders, slow worms and other small creatures.

However, even if your garden is a neat, tidy place without any trees, there will always be some wildlife present. All gardens have soil, of course, and this is where many of the smaller creatures of the garden live. Earthworms are the gardener's friend, for they help mix the earth together, and create air passages for the roots of plants. Other animals of the soil include beetles and their larvae, centipedes and millipedes, and ants. If you carefully lift a large stone in the garden you will often see ants scuttling about, for they often build their nests under stones.

Sometimes gardeners find large heaps of soil on their carefully tended lawns. These are caused by moles, which burrow through the earth and push the soil they have excavated up on to the grass.

Hidden among the fallen leaves or creeping between the stems of the flowers in the flower beds are other animals such as slugs and snails.

Many of the creatures of the garden are very secretive. They remain hidden from view and only emerge from the safety of their hiding places to feed at night. Birds, however, are among the easiest of garden animals to see. We can encourage them by planting trees, or by growing bushes with berries which they can eat in the autumn. In winter, a bird feeding table will also attract hungry flocks, eager for something to eat.

Wild plants, too, will find their way into the garden. The plants we call weeds are really just wild flowers growing uninvited. In autumn, mushrooms and toadstools will appear mysteriously from the ground, and lichens, mosses and other lowly plants will soon colonize rocks.

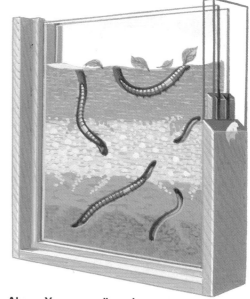

Above: You can easily make a wormery yourself. The one shown here is made from two sheets of glass with soil sandwiched between them, but a jam jar containing some moist soil and a few leaves is just as good. Watch the earthworms mix the soil as they burrow through it.

Below: Some common garden animals. Many of the smaller creatures spend the day hidden under stones or leaves, but at night they are much more active and can easily be seen with the aid of a torch.

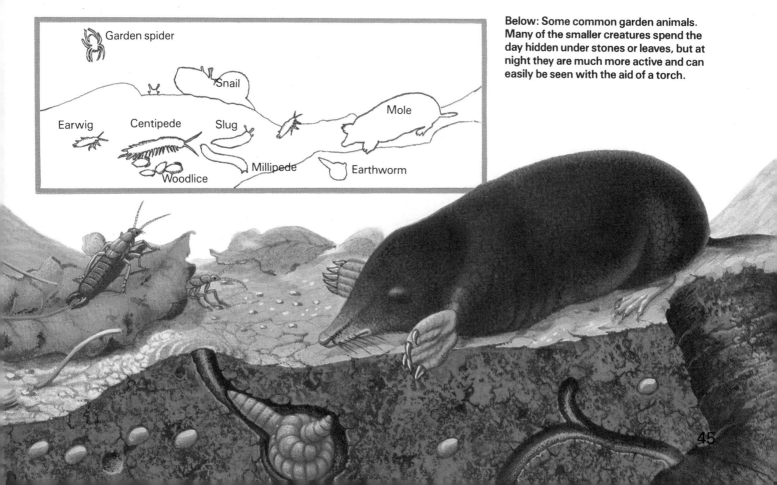

45

Index

46

Illustrators
Mike Atkinson, Jim Dugdale, Ron Jobson, Linden Artists Ltd.,
John Marshall, Bernard Robinson, Frederick St. Ward,
Mike Saunders and David Wright.

Cover illustrations by
Graham Austin/Garden Studio

Copyright © 1991 Cliveden Press.
All rights reserved. Published in
Great Britain by Cliveden Press,
an Egmont Company, Egmont House,
PO Box 111, Great Ducie Street,
Manchester M60 3BL.

Printed in Singapore.

ISBN 0 7498 0395 9

Reprinted 1992